# ARTISTS' HOMES

# ARTISTS' HOMES

## Live/Work Spaces for Modern Makers

Tom Harford Thompson

*with 350 illustrations*

Thames & Hudson

It all started on a sunny day in a café in Lewes, East Sussex, where I first met Elain McAlpine, the editor of this book. It was only a cursory meeting, as she was actually having lunch with someone else. A few details were exchanged, and I received a call to have a meeting with her to discuss possible projects. The result is *Artists' Homes*.

I would like to thank, first of all, my wife Ruth, who has listened, helped and been an invaluable source of advice. She has also been an editor par excellence of my initial scribblings. Secondly, I want to thank Elain McAlpine, who has been a brilliant editor and a very tactful navigator and pilot of this book. She has steered it through every stage, and had faith in my ideas from the very beginning. I would also like to thank the designer Avni Patel, who has taken over two dozen CDs of photographs and turned them into what you are holding now.

And lastly, I would like to thank all the people who have generously given up their time and allowed me into their homes to snoop around with my camera. Thank you.

This book is for Ruth, George and Flora

On the cover: *Front, clockwise from top right* The studio of potter Chris Lewis; the tools of potter Sarah Walton's trade; storage solutions in Viv and Ben English's house, 'Farthings'; *Back, left to right* A corner of artist Billy Childish's studio in Kent; the kitchen at Breaky Bottom, in the Sussex Downs.

On p. 2: The magnificent garden outside Chris Lewis's studio.

*Artists' Homes: Live/Work Spaces for Modern Makers*
© 2018 Thames & Hudson Ltd, London
Text © 2018 Tom Harford Thompson

Photographs © 2018 Tom Harford Thompson

First published in 2018 in the United States of America by Thames & Hudson Inc., 500 Fifth Avenue, New York, New York 10110

www.thamesandhudsonusa.com

Library of Congress Control Number 2018932291

ISBN 978-0-500-02132-3

Printed in China by RR Donnelley

# Contents

# Introduction

I AM A JUNKIE FOR INTERIORS MAGAZINES. My heart still skips a beat when the grey plastic parcel drops through my letterbox, and I know that the latest issue of *World of Interiors* has arrived. Beautiful homes for beautiful people. But as much as I like being inspired by the photographs, I am often left wondering about the people who live in these perfect houses. What is their story? Who are they, and do they really live like this?

*Artists' Homes* goes behind the gloss to reveal the true habitat of the artist, and the workings of the creative life. Each space is exactly how I found it, and nothing has been 'dressed' or styled, no matter how much the occupants protested about wanting to tidy up. Like a portrait painter, a photographer attempts to reveal the real person behind the façade – or, in the case of this book, behind the front door. To do this, I have focused on the details inside people's homes, whether a notice-board in the kitchen or keys on the mantelpiece, or a dressing table with framed photographs and out-of-date invitations crowding its surface. Some may dismiss these details as just so much clutter, but they often tell us more about the people who live there than their choice of sofa or new car.

Although I am constantly inspired by the way my artist friends have designed their homes, their workshops and studios can be just as revealing, with an air of unconscious ease that comes from practical use. Their function informs their beauty – an extension of William Morris's oft-quoted stricture to have nothing in your home that is not beautiful or useful. This can be applied to workspaces as well, from James Mitchell's classic-car business in the blast house of a disused airfield (p. 132) to Ian Hatton's motorcycle workshop in the Sussex countryside (p. 178) and Liam Watson's analogue recording studio in East London (p. 170).

Opposite:
This outbuilding, resembling a miniature cricket pavilion, is used as the HQ of the Indian-club society founded by Billy Childish.

People can be less precious in their studios, which, consequently, become more of a natural reflection of their occupants than the houses themselves.

The patina acquired by the wear and tear of people going about their daily business creates an atmosphere that is impossible to replicate, and certainly cannot be bought from a shop specializing in 'distressed' furniture. It shows what really goes on behind closed doors, the shortcuts people take and the sometimes unexpected ways they use objects: the shabby chair that's always used as a coat stand, for example; the child's toy that has been commandeered as a paperweight; or the valuable bronze statuette that has found a new role as a home for the remote control.

In the homes of those creatives with young children, the evidence of home life is even more on view. In the home of Anthony and Lori Inglis Hall (p. 88), a row of babies' bibs dries above the fireplace, while in Billy Childish's kitchen, examples of his daughter's artwork are pinned up on the walls beneath the Union Jack bunting (p. 10). This evidence of use is a vital part of the look of the interior of a house or studio (or of any space – I was very tempted to include a friend's 1952 Land Rover, complete with battle-scarred paintwork).

Such spaces are usually immune to fashion and have been added to gradually over the years, with little planning or forethought. The occupants, their friends, relations and casual acquaintances have all added to the flotsam and jetsam accumulated over the decades, with each addition bringing its own history, waiting to be rediscovered by a future inhabitant. The result is something that is imperfect and tells a story about real homes and the creative lives lived within them – a story that I hope this book manages to convey.

Opposite:
The hallway in muralist Alan Dodd's
17th-century house, known locally
as 'Mustard Pot Hall'.

# Billy Childish
## ARTIST

Billy Childish – artist, musician, agent provocateur – has been working on the margins for a long time. He initially came to prominence as a member of the band Thee Milkshakes, once part of the Medway punk scene – the British answer to the American garage bands of the 1960s. Having been thrown out of St Martins School of Art in the late 1970s, he ploughed a lonely furrow over the following decades, painting and writing poetry.

Artistic recognition for his work finally came with a solo show at the Institute of Contemporary Arts in London in 2010. Now internationally famous, with art agents in several countries, Billy has stayed close to his roots. His studio is in the Ropery at Chatham Dockyard in Kent, where he started out as a 16-year-old apprentice stonemason. Every part of his working process is considered, even down to the overall he wears: an original Royal Flying Corps specimen from the First World War. The look is completed with a 1930s trilby hat and carefully styled moustache.

An extension of this cultivated artistic persona is Billy's home, a beautiful Victorian townhouse outside Rochester. It once belonged to Oswald Short of Short Brothers, a local company notable chiefly for their designs for flying boats, produced from the 1920s to the 1950s. Billy is proud of this local connection, and is keen to promote this less familiar side of the area's history. This is an artist who lives with an ear constantly half-cocked to history, mixing his discoveries with a personal blend of rock 'n' roll and paint to produce something extraordinary.

**Opposite:**
Above the Aga is one of the many items about the house relating to local manufacturers Short Brothers. At the bottom of the garden is a stretch of river where Oswald Short, who used to own the house, and his brother Eustace tested their flying boats.

**Above:**
In the kitchen, Billy's daughter's paintings provide a pleasing contrast to the crisp, green kitchen cabinets. Many of the colours have been chosen deliberately for their prewar, colonial feel, accentuated by the Union Jack bunting. Billy particularly likes the look of the 1930s, which is carried throughout the house.

**Overleaf:**
In much of the building, the plaster on the walls has been left unpainted (p. 14) – a conscious decision to ensure that Billy's artwork doesn't have to compete with paint colours. Another view of the kitchen with its scrubbed pine table (p. 15), whose white-painted legs sit on top of a 1930s-inspired geometric rug. Above the doorway is yet more memorabilia from the Short Brothers firm – a carved wooden plaque made to commemorate the building of one of the flying boats.

**Opposite:**
The bedroom is an eclectic mix of styles, from the Art Nouveau bedside lamp to the Airfix Spitfire and Messerschmitt Me-109 kit models, hangovers from Billy's childhood, on top of the shelves. In the cupboard is an example of the military clothing collected by Billy since he was a teenager, which can be found all over the house.

**Above:**
One of Billy's paintings hangs above a Victorian daybed in the spare bedroom. While visiting Billy and his family, I spent several hours in the studio, watching the artist at work. He starts with a charcoal sketch, which is then quickly filled in with oil paint. Speed is of the essence, and the finished work is often completed in under three hours.

**Previous pages:**
Billy's study (p. 16), with ex-army campaign shorts on view. The fireplace is original to the house, and is surrounded by lovely Delft tiles decorated in simple yet charming motifs. On the mantelpiece is yet more Short Brothers memorabilia: a cast aluminium model of a flying boat. Above it hangs a black-and-white photograph of another one.

This charcoal drawing in the spare bedroom (p. 17) is a good example of the loose style Billy adopts when at the preparatory stages of painting. It is pinned onto a tongue-and-groove wall, a contrast to the rough, unpainted wall next to it.

**Opposite:**
The paint-spattered floorboards in Billy's studio in the Ropery at Chatham Dockyard hint at the palpable feeling of toil and sweat within its walls. This square space, which he shares with a fellow artist, is above an enormous room, nearly 100 m (330 ft) in length, where rope for the Royal Navy was once made.

**Above:**
Billy at work on a painting that started off as a photograph, before being roughly transferred onto canvas with charcoal (left). He works quickly and in silence, periodically stepping back to examine his work – propped up on two chairs and leaned back against the wall – while sipping from a mug of green tea.

**Overleaf:**
Paintings are stacked against the wall, before being packaged and sent to Billy's dealer (p. 22). Preferring to work with oils, rather than acrylic, which he feels has too modern a finish (p. 23), he references the past in his paintings, mixing up all of his influences until something unique emerges.

# Jonny Hannah
## ARTIST

Jonny Hannah lives in a 1980s terraced house on a quiet suburban street in Southampton, on the south coast. It has an anonymous, workmanlike feel to it, a quality that he deliberately looked for during his search for a home. This anonymity was important, as it provides the backdrop to his artistic imagination.

Jonny grew up in a similar house in Scotland in the 1970s and remembers it being steeped in 1950s Americana – cowboy films, Levis, Coca-Cola – an antidote to the ordinary suburban town. During his childhood, he absorbed his parents' passion for Hollywood glamour, and later created his own fantasy place, 'Darktown' – an American term that describes the end of town where the poor and marginalized tend to congregate – or, as Jonny puts it, 'where the freaks live'.

There is a thread of the surreal running through his world. On entering the garden, a robotic voice booms out: 'Warning! You are under surveillance.' On closer inspection, it turns out that this comes from a security camera, placed high up on the next-door neighbour's wall, and is activated every time someone enters the garden. To most people, this would be a serious infringement of personal space, but to Jonny, it is all part of the narrative of Darktown.

Nothing escapes his fertile imagination – including a family car, recently bought online and decorated in his distinctive style. Christened the 'Darktown Turbo Taxi' and covered in advertisements for the town's 'businesses', it is yet another layer of the fully realized vision of his imaginary world.

This page:

The handpainted house number (above) gives the first hint that this is not your normal suburban dwelling. Jonny's extensive vinyl collection (above left), including a rare LP by Mark Wilson's band The Mob (see p. 254), is put to good use, as he often DJs at various events. The shed at the bottom of the garden (left) does double-duty as his studio.

Opposite:

The Darktown taxi, a bog-standard Toyota that Jonny bought for £800 on Gumtree. The idea for painting it originally came from his agent. Since then, the car has come in useful as a promotional device, making appearances at various printmakers' exhibitions and fairs – driven by Jonny's wife, as he cannot drive.

# Peter Hall

## VINTNER

Lying at the heart of the Sussex Downs, Breaky Bottom Vineyard is owned, managed and farmed by Peter Hall, who arrived here in 1965, fresh from agricultural college in Newcastle. At first he lived in nearby Brighton, getting up at 5am to take the first of two buses to Breaky Bottom, where he would wait with the other farm hands to be given a day's work. Tiring of this journey, he asked if he could live on the farm, in what was a derelict shack, home only to sheep. An old sofa was the only evidence that the building had ever been occupied.

When Peter moved in, the house had no electricity and only a standpipe for water. His first purchase was, he says, 'optimistic' – it was a double bed. This was delivered on a Saturday night and he spent the evening face-down on the mattress, listening to classical music. Disturbed by the sound of banging, he felt hands pushing him into the mattress and grabbed hold of one of them, which returned his grip, squeezing tightly. It seems he had met the house's resident ghost.

While working at the farm, Peter met Diana, the farmer's daughter. A few years later, married and with a young family, it seemed a natural, if brave, step to move permanently into the house. With a French mother who was an exceptional cook, and a grandfather who had been a famous restaurateur in Soho, Peter had food and wine in his blood. In 1974, on realizing that the local climate was very similar to the Loire Valley, the couple decided to plant their own vineyard. Breaky Bottom has since developed into a highly regarded winery and has helped to pave the way for the popularity of English wine.

**Opposite:**
Peter's beautiful kitchen, complete with a well-used cooker. Who doesn't enjoy looking at a kitchen that is used and loved? Whether it is the burnt pans or the half-used bottles of oil, it is the evidence of work that is fascinating. The kitchen was built by Peter's son Toby, a skilled cabinetmaker and timber-framer.

**Above:**
The kitchen is housed in an extension, also built by Toby, which has almost doubled the size of the building. The earthenware mugs, plates and tureens, along with the wall-mounted wooden shelf, all contribute to the handmade look of the kitchen joinery.

**Overleaf:**
A simple arrangement of alliums (p. 38), freshly picked from the garden and placed in a vintage bottle, which itself may well have been dug up in the garden, next to a pair of beeswax candles. The long kitchen table is an antique and looks totally at home in the new extension. Peter's second wife, Chris, is an artist and has her own studio in the house (p. 39). The photograph is of a friend of hers, taken in the 1960s. Chris is very much a part of the local artistic community, and can often be found helping out behind the scenes at various exhibitions.

**Above:**
The various objects gathered together on an antique side table in the kitchen have resulted in a charming still life. The lamp base, made by a local artist, and the handthrown plates are the fruits of a lifetime of collecting and visiting local art fairs.

**Opposite:**
The precision of the newly built bookcases provides a contrast to the Victorian ladderback chair. The bookcases were also built by Toby, who as an unruly 16-year-old schoolboy was sent to a specialist cabinetmaker in Buckinghamshire to help get him back on the straight and narrow. The pots and jugs are part of Chris's collection.

**Overleaf:**
Opposite the house are various farm buildings that date from the 1960s. Part of the barn has been divided up and is used as artists' studios, one of which is used by Peter's daughter Kate, who works as an interior designer and is also an accomplished sculptor (p. 42). Both Kate and her twin sister Emily, a skilled weaver, quilter and design teacher, grew up riding horses bareback across the Sussex Downs. Her riding has been curtailed somewhat since having children, so modelling a horse is probably the nearest she will get to one for the time being (p. 43).

**Above:**
Kate specializes in sculpting heads or busts (left); a recent commission was for a high-profile Labour MP for the University of Sussex. On her desk can be found all sorts of objects (right), chosen for their tactile qualities, which will find their way somehow into the next sculpture.

**Opposite:**
Seen on a cold, wintry day, the studio has been cobbled together from 'found' objects, including old Crittal windows and a door from another building. The net effect of this magpie approach is often more sympathetic to its new setting than something custom-built for the job.

# Lisa Smallpeice

## ARTIST

Lisa Smallpeice first appeared on my doorstep about 20 years ago, looking for a room to rent. After looking around and making a few sarcastic remarks, she moved in. Fast-forward a few years, and she is now living on a farm with her husband Toby and two children. Lisa studied at the Brighton School of Art, and her paintings are much in demand. Her artistic genesis began via a tried and tested path – drawing her left hand – and there is always a quirky detail in the way she puts things together, from her outfits to a vegan meal.

Ten years ago, Lisa and Toby decided to leave Brighton and bought a farm, deep in the English countryside. It was love at first sight, and was bought in less time than it takes to buy a pair of jeans. The house itself was added to, although it took a number of attempts and four architects to get the design right. Today, the farm is home to several businesses, and no potential venture escapes the couple's entrepreneurial ambitions, from producing their own craft beer (Gun Brewery) to using the natural spring water found on the farm in a range of beauty products (Amly Botanicals).

Lisa and Toby also provide custom wedding packages for couples who want a rustic but romantic wedding experience, and offer accommodation at the farm's holiday cottages, converted from the old cowshed and granary. Whether working as an artist or creator of perfumes, or simply employed on the farm, nothing escapes Lisa's artistic eye.

**Opposite:**
Lisa's studio, covered in wallpaper with a leaf motif, is tacked onto the side of the house, with a glass roof to provide plenty of satisfying top light. She devotes much of her spare time to trawling auctions and junk shops for pictures and paintings to provide inspiration for her own work.

**Above:**
In front of the studio is a walled garden. Lisa cheerfully admits that she is not in the least green-fingered, so a gardener is employed to do the heavy work, with Lisa very much in charge of operations.

**Previous pages:**
The land that came with the property is put to good use in many ways. The natural spring water found on the site is used for Toby's beer business and in Lisa's beauty products, while the farm's outbuildings have been restored and are now used as holiday lets and for the wedding business.

Today, the farm is a good example of self-sufficiency, with everything working together and feeding back into other parts of the business.

**Opposite:**
A chair in Lisa's studio, with a handknitted blanket thrown across it, sits in front of an exterior wall of the house. The chair may not be an object of beauty, but it is comfortable and ideal for curling up in while looking out onto the walled garden, preferably while waiting for some artistic divine inspiration.

**Above:**
In the living room is an assortment of paintings and old photograph albums collected by Lisa. A favourite haunt is Watsons auction house in Heathfield, with a proper old-school café that is especially welcome after an early morning of searching through auction lots.

**Above:**
The house is essentially a large, two-storey cottage. Above the fireplace in the sitting room is some casually draped ribbon bunting, accessorized with a few works of folk art from Lisa's collection.

**Opposite:**
In another corner of the sitting room, different patterns and textures have been put together in a pleasing way, from the colours of the cushions to the fabric wall hanging with its 1970s feel. Unusually, the wooden base of the standard lamp has been wrapped in paper.

**Overleaf:**
Toby has erected quite a few shed-like structures about the property, which the couple use for events. In one of these, decorations lie abandoned after a party (p. 56). The untreated wood panelling in the kitchen (p. 57) has been done in a deliberately roughshod fashion, giving the interior of the house a homespun quality.

**Above:**
One of the rooms in the holiday
cottage, a surprisingly spacious
converted cowshed (left). Lisa has
teamed a 1960s bentwood chair with
an old wooden trestle table (right) –
an unlikely pairing that seems
to work.

**Opposite:**
The large kitchen can easily
accommodate a dinner party
for 12. As with every cottage,
however, storage is an issue, so
this freestanding cupboard, painted
in various shades of grey, is ideal.
The red handpainted chair adds
just the right splash of colour.

**Opposite:**

Considering the amount of land that came with the property, the house itself is very modest in scale. Although it was virtually taken apart and rebuilt from scratch, the cottage has a deliberately unpolished appearance, giving the impression that it has always looked that way.

**Above:**

If a bit of alfresco camping is what you're after, you've come to the right place. There are also a number of shepherd huts providing accommodation. Pictured is the area where campers perform their morning ablutions, at a period-correct butler's sink in the perfect rustic setting.

# Sarah Walton

## POTTER

Sarah Walton lives at the foot of the Sussex Downs in an old estate cottage bought by her parents as a holiday home after the Second World War (the family lived the rest of the year in London). After Sarah inherited it, she decided to make it her own home, with the addition of a ceramics studio.

Inside, practical decisions have been married to aesthetic ones, all of which have added to the house's charm and character. In the larder, shelves are carefully lined with sticky-back plastic in blue gingham, setting off Sarah's collection of crockery to perfection, while her father's various Heath Robinson carpentry solutions include pegs that have been sharpened to prevent coats from falling off.

Sarah attended Chelsea School of Art in the 1960s, and originally wanted to be a painter. Following a bereavement in the family, she decided to change tack and train as a nurse, but after five years of nursing, she began to think about returning to art school to study pottery. Sarah believes that her experience as a nurse of handling and working so closely with people has translated into working in three dimensions with clay. After a period of experimentation, she narrowed her output down to exquisite bird baths, which she sells at her open studios and at the Chelsea Flower Show.

Sarah's art is all-encompassing. She guiltily admits that even at church, when she is meant to be praying, she is often distracted by the stone coins around the casement windows, wondering how the effect could be translated into one of her sculptures.

In the bedroom, the simple
arrangement of plates on the wall
is a soothing backdrop to the black-
and-white photographs that crowd
the dressing table, creating an
unintentional and unexpected still
life. Sarah uses the small sculptures
as inspiration for future work, and
lights the white candle each night
before going to bed.

**Above:**
A row of well-thumbed art books
in the bedroom. Throughout the
house is evidence of Sarah's interest
in medieval pottery, Neolithic art,
Western painting and the arts of
Mesopotamia and South East Asia.
The charming pencil sketches also
hint at her previous life at art college
as a painter.

**Overleaf:**
Sometimes it is the smallest details
that reveal the most. Hanging above
a shelf with some of Sarah's work
displayed on top is a painting whose
simple, monochrome palette echoes
the raw subtlety of the unglazed bowl
in front of it (p. 66). One of her pencil
sketches hangs in an alcove beneath
the stairs (p. 67); above are some
mounted tiles, also made by Sarah.

This page:
In Sarah's kitchen, an old cupboard above the cooker acts as a visual diary, with notes and recipes attached to the insides of the doors. None of the plates or cutlery matches, but still creates a pleasing effect.

Opposite:
Nearly all of the plates, bowls and mugs in Sarah's cupboard have been made by her. Many are the result of idle experimentation, but together they form an archive of her work. Each year, they are pressed into service at her annual open days.

**Opposite:**
Sarah specializes in monumental bird baths, examples of which can be seen in her studio. The table is an old one that had apparently finished its usefulness in her house, and given a new lease of life in the less precious environment of the studio.

**Above:**
The studio is a simple breeze-block structure that is separate to the house. Inside is one main area with good light, where Sarah sculpts the clay. Towards the back of the space are various drying and storage racks.

**Overleaf:**
Sarah has drawn outlines around some of her most-used tools on the wall of the studio, so that their absence can be easily spotted (p. 72) – an old mechanic's trick. Well-worn shirts and a denim apron that Sarah wears while working hang on a makeshift coat rack (p. 73).

**Opposite:**
One of Sarah's terracotta garden pots, leaning against a wall of the studio, acts as a giant container for another, smaller pot. It has aged beautifully, covered with lichen, and acquired a patina that plastic containers cannot match. A rickety bench provides a spot for Sarah to sit and admire her garden, which is peppered with her bird baths.

**Above:**
Along the side return of the cottage is a wooden construction that looks as if it has been added on at some point in the distant past (left). It is a square room that Sarah uses for displaying smaller pieces of work and to note down customers' details at her open days. From her front garden, she has an uninterrupted view of the countryside (right).

# Viv & Ben English
## PUBLICAN & TATTOOIST

I have often walked past 'Farthings', pausing to wonder what the house was like inside. One day, while chatting at the school gates with Viv English, whose son is in the same class as mine, she told me that she and her husband Ben, a tattoo artist, had just bought it. Viv has a track record of interesting purchases: she bought a pub in Lewes when she was just 25, while also working as a midwife – not, I imagine, a common mix of occupations.

Over 40 people had wanted to buy the house, but after a whittling-down process that included face-to-face interviews, Viv and Ben were chosen as the new owners – entrusted by the children of the previous occupants to keep it in the same spirit as their parents. The house dates back to 1940, when it was designed by a young architect straight out of college, and has been added to, bit by bit, over the years as the family grew.

Viv and Ben have embarked on a sympathetic restoration of the house, which is in what can be called 'barn-find' condition, staying true to the architect's original intentions while also bringing it up to a standard fit for family life and that banks will agree to mortgage. The hand of the designer is still evident throughout the building, and the atmosphere is enhanced by the presence of many of the former owners' possessions – including paintings and even a pair of looms. The garden, too, is a wilderness waiting to be reclaimed, with large cages full of overgrown, tangled raspberries and vegetable beds, half-buried beneath a year's growth of grass. This is a period gem just waiting to be given a future.

**Opposite:**

The garden, before the clippers got to it – surely a gardener's dream! This lovely space was once much loved, but has been left to run wild and go to seed, quietly biding its time before the next owner puts their stamp on it. Fruit cages and vegetable beds indicate past cultivation and hint at treasures waiting to be rediscovered.

**Above:**

The addition of a wooden conservatory gives the house an American West Coast feel that is slightly at odds with its English pastoral setting. The house is a complete time capsule, and is exactly as the couple found it when they bought it. Houseplants seem a bit unfashionable at the moment – perhaps they are due a revival?

**Overleaf:**

The main living space, with its monumental stone fireplace (p. 80). The well-worn chair and rush matting look as if they have been there since the middle of the last century. The exposed brick wall has been painted black (p. 81) and, along with the woven baskets and floor covering, is in keeping with the house's vintage vibe.

**Above:**

The many objects on display are further proof of artistic minds at work (left); unusual sculptures can even be found on the walls (right). There is an emphasis throughout the house on natural materials, from practical floor coverings to more decorative items, including handmade pots and arrangements of dried flowers.

**Opposite:**

Hessian walls in the living room – surely the days of white walls are numbered. Running one's hands along tactile walls is an experience we have not enjoyed since the 1960s and '70s. The chairs are also from the '60s, and echo the colour palette of the tribal implements hanging on the wall.

**Overleaf:**

A view through the internal casement window to the conservatory (p. 84), which may have to be knocked down as it does not conform to modern building regulations. In the same room is a slightly wonky bookshelf with a Cézanne-inspired painting above (p. 85).

**Above:**
A colonial-style chair, painted
in white gloss paint and without
its seat, looks at ease in this
conservatory setting, with hats
on the walls that are there for
practical purposes, rather than
for effect. The exposed brick walls
are painted with the same paint.

**Opposite:**
Also in the conservatory is this
circular rattan chair and matching
side table, both from the 1960s. The
walls at the back of the house are
filled with hay – an exciting and
ecological idea at the time the house
was built, but nearly 80 years later
they have become infested with
creatures and insects.

# Anthony & Lori Inglis Hall
## VINTAGE & ANTIQUES DEALERS

Anthony and Lori Inglis Hall both look as if they have stepped out of photographs from another era. Anthony could be a gentleman artist, reclining in a deck chair at Charleston farmhouse in the 1930s, while Lori's appearance is more 1960s and folksy. They are both interested in clothes, but ultimately it is the overall look, whether of an interior or a garden, that inspires them.

Anthony works as an antiques dealer, but has other strings to his bow. He studied at Chelsea School of Art and produces beautiful pictures cut from paper. Lori, whom he met while walking the dog in a London park, juggles running her vintage clothing business with bringing up their two small boys. Both have a great eye, so I was intrigued to find out why they had moved into this rather unprepossessing house. The reason was straightforward: the estate was keen to have a young couple with children, as the local school was very small and much in need of new pupils.

The house can be found down a long track (dodging a few sheep on the way), and over a railway bridge. It is in an idyllic setting, with barely any evidence of civilization on the horizon, and was an ideal blank canvas for the couple's fertile imagination. Anthony specializes in transforming mundane houses with original features, adding his own details to create interiors that look as if they have always been that way. In one room, he removed the floors and laid oak floorboards and terracotta tiles, revealing some competent carpentry skills, and introduced quirky mouldings. The result is a charming house that belies its exterior.

**Opposite:**
Anthony's workshop. Most of the objects that he buys are from France, and destined for an auction house that specializes in French decorative antiques. There is a running joke between us that he buys things in France that I buy in England, and promptly return to a house I have in Normandy.

**Above:**
A handpainted cupboard and vintage garden chair inside the small conservatory (left). The choice of plants reflects Lori's influence, as she is the person in charge of gardening decisions in the family.

**Overleaf:**
In the living room, the couple's eldest child watches television; a crocheted throw flung over the sofa gives it a folksy feel (p. 92). The herringbone woodblock flooring looks as if it has been down for years, but in reality Anthony laid it only a few months ago. The fireplace is accessorized with china figurines and a row of drying bibs (p. 93).

**Below:**

In one corner of the living room, an ancient French club chair, found by Anthony on his travels, is teamed with a pair of Matisse-inspired curtains. Anthony ran a small record label at one time, and some of its releases can be found among his extensive vinyl collection.

**Opposite:**

Lori collects vintage fabrics, which are used to great effect throughout the house. Here, she has added an antimacassar from the 1930s to the back of a sofa, along with a Mexican-inspired cushion.

**Opposite:**
Stored on top of the trestle-style table in the kitchen, painted and renovated by Anthony, are a metal classical urn and one of his own sculptures, set against an antique Japanese-influenced wall hanging. Lori's vintage sewing box sits on the floor beside it.

**Above:**
In the bedroom, the Japanese theme is continued, with another wall hanging and one of Lori's decorative fans propped up on the dresser, as well as the carved, bamboo-like headboard of the couple's four-poster bed.

**Opposite:**
Above a cupboard rubbed down
to the bare wood by Anthony is an
antique silvered mirror and metal
urn. Next to it, a leaded mirror gives
the impression that it is a window
into the next room. The plates on
the wall are some of Lori's finds,
discovered while searching for
vintage clothing.

**Above:**
The function for this room has yet to
be decided. The room, including the
bare bricks, has been painted white,
prior to hanging vintage wallpaper.
The house's many fireplaces have all
had to be opened up after years of
neglect.

# Carolyn Trant

## ARTIST

Carolyn Trant, an artist who produces limited-edition books, describes herself as a frustrated poet, having been persuaded as a student to pursue painting instead of writing. She trained at the Slade in the 1960s, and was taught by Euan Uglow (my favourite painter, although when I mention this she pulls a face – Uglow's insistence on laborious measuring techniques nearly put Carolyn off drawing for life). Another teacher was Peggy Angus, whose home 'Furlongs' was a retreat for a circle of artists that included, among others, Eric Ravilious.

When Carolyn and her husband Peter first met, Peter had hair to his waist and was wearing a pair of John Lennon glasses. He weighed eight stone and had just got back from a walking tour of Syria. Carolyn, with her shock of red hair and layers of clothes, cut a similarly bohemian figure. They are both creative people, with Peter running a printing shop (Tom Paine Printing Press) that has a letterpress, which is often called into service for printing his wife's books.

Carolyn describes the process of book-making as 'creating a time capsule', and the couple's home – an elegant Victorian townhouse in one of the loveliest crescents in Lewes – has many of the same qualities. Every nook and cranny has been packed with art, potential art, and bits and pieces that might one day become art. No room is sacred, and the kitchen houses an enormous printing press and trays of formaldehyde. The result, with its layers upon layers of books and general clutter, is a creative environment ('a creative slum', Peter says), which Carolyn thrives on.

**Below:**

Each room in the house contains teetering piles of books and paintings – an archaeologist's dream. 'Minimalism' is not a concept that the couple have ever subscribed to.

**Opposite:**

The kitchen is in the basement, where light is at a premium, with a door opening out onto a small, square garden. Piled up next to and on top of the antique pine dresser are bags of the walnuts that Carolyn buys in bulk and lives on.

**Opposite:**
Throughout the house (including here, in the living room), the walls are covered not just with Carolyn's own art, but with other people's work, as well. There is no theme or focus to her collecting, and the overall feeling is of someone with extremely eclectic tastes.

**Above:**
Everywhere you look are objects in seemingly incongruous settings. In the front room, a sculpture of a figure crowned with antlers perches atop a child's high chair.

**Above:**
This room was once one of the children's bedrooms (with the toy tiger just visible on the left a bit of a giveaway). The yellow walls and blue skirting boards are left over from the early 1990s.

**Opposite:**
A collection of rocks and driftwood has found a home on the window sill of the landing, while a stack of paintings leans patiently against the wall, waiting for some free space to be found. They could be waiting a very long time, as every available surface in the house has already been covered in artwork.

**Overleaf:**
In the kitchen (p. 108), a lot more happens than just cooking. A large printing press sits in the middle of the room, and pages from one of Carolyn's books can often be found drying on a makeshift clothesline.

# Chris Lewis

## POTTER

The last time I saw Chris Lewis, he was sporting an elastic surgical belt, wrapped tightly around his waist – apparently an accessory that one acquires after a lifetime of lugging heavy ceramic pots around. I was at his studio to buy a huge garden urn I had spied at one of his open-house weekends. It had exploded when it came out of the kiln, and a young apprentice had offered to cement it back together. The result is now a thing of fractured beauty.

Chris, too, originally came here as an assistant – to the house's then owner, potter Ursula Mommens. (Ursula, apart from her artistic achievements, was astonishingly well connected: she was a direct descendant of Josiah Wedgwood, the great-granddaughter of Charles Darwin, a relation of Ralph Vaughan Williams, and wife of the painter Julian Trevelyan and later the sculptor Norman Mommens.) Upon arriving in 1976, Chris shared the house and studio with Ursula, and when she died at the age of 101, he and his partner Rachel inherited them both.

One of the first changes Chris made was to the kiln, replacing it with one that keeps the firewood in direct contact with the pots during firing. This gives them their distinctive archaeological look. Rachel, too, has made changes, particularly in the large, sloping garden. The effect is enchanting, with Chris's pots dotted about the raised vegetable beds, like ancient sarsen stones. The studio and garden are usually open to the public in May, with the couple's sublime brownies served beneath apple trees festooned with clematis.

**Opposite:**
The side return of Chris's studio, one of the many buildings that he and Rachel refurbished after Ursula's death. This is where he shapes the pots at the wheel, before storing them for firing in the kiln, which is in a separate building behind the studio. To the right of it is one of Chris's finished pots.

**This page:**
The garden is on a steep incline, with the studio at the bottom of the slope – not ideal gardening terrain, perhaps, but it works perfectly as a background to the couple's open-house weekends.

Previous pages:
Chris stores all of the 'seconds' –
pots that may have gone wrong in
the firing process and are deemed to
be less than perfect – in one of the
unrestored barns (p. 114). More pots
that have not made the grade (p. 115),
and have been unceremoniously
dumped on a shelf.

This page:
These clay pipes (above) are related
to the firing process. Chris used the
same wood-fired kiln for over 20
years, before switching over to one
that uses a new technique, in which
the pots are actually in contact with
the ash and embers of the fire.

Opposite:
A teetering pile of bases, onto which
Chris throws the clay when starting
a pot. Next to it is a jar containing
the clay-encrusted tools he uses to
shape or mark the clay as it turns on
the wheel. One implement appears
to be a sponge fastened to the end
of a stick.

**Opposite:**
Everything in the studio is covered in a fine powder of dust, which gives the room a wonderful dry, almost baked, patina. All of the tools that Chris uses when marking the rotating pots, whether a feather or a wooden spatula, are made from natural materials in keeping with the slow rhythm of the making process.

**Above:**
The house was originally split into two flats when Chris lived here with Ursula. He and Rachel have since knocked the building back into one home, adding a room onto the side. They use this as a gallery for exhibiting paintings that are visually complementary to Chris's ceramic work.

**Overleaf:**
The garden in full bloom at the height of summer. It is a work in progress, with new paths and plants appearing every year. Chris not only makes pots, but also ceramic seats, which are placed around the garden to make the most of the views. At the top of the garden is the most perfect wall, which is actually the side of a neighbour's ancient barn, made from the local stone. It acts as a perfect foil for Rachel's shrubs and trees.

# Patrick Hall
## ANTIQUES DEALER

Patrick Hall, with his rosy complexion, has the look of someone who has lived well. He grew up with good food (his mother was an exceptional cook), and it has always been a major feature of his trips to France for his business. As a result of these frequent forays, he has created a detailed map of the country, with all of his favourite boulangeries and charcuteries, discovered over many years, marked out.

Patrick stumbled into the world of antiques by accident. He went to agricultural college for a year, but was lured away from a life on the farm by his uncle, who ran an antiques shop in Bristol. Over the years, he has spent much of his time driving around the French countryside searching for antiques to sell. A friend who has known him for many years said that he is constantly amazed at the kinds of things he will buy – he was once found in a Le Mans café trying to cajole six local men into lifting a huge vintage lathe into the back of his truck.

Patrick's future wife Didi was a friend of the family and at boarding school. When he was in the area, he would smuggle her out of school and she would join him on his hunting trips. Later, Didi worked in the costume department of a theatre, but with a growing family to look after, she decided to help Patrick full-time with the business. Now that their three children have grown up, there is an air of calm about the farmhouse. Didi is quietly doing needlepoint in her sewing room, while Patrick is busy in the couple's huge barn, surrounded by the old tractors and speedboats found while on his travels, fixing his finds up for auction.

**Opposite:**
The barn is testament to Patrick's eclectic taste. Crammed inside it are a pair of fire dogs, a stuffed wild boar on wheels, a cast-iron fire backplate and a set of antlers on the wall. Most of his finds are sold at specialist auctions: he has concentrated his efforts on various areas over the years, including antique corkscrews.

**Above:**
The barn is stuffed to the rafters, quite literally, with objects that Patrick has discovered (right). Most of these items, such as this rocking horse (left), will need some repairs or restoration – a task Patrick will take on himself, thanks to his detailed knowledge of how an object should look after years in the antiques trade.

**Above:**
In Patrick's well-organized workshop, old tobacco tins have been commandeered for housing drill bits, screws and other small items (left). Beneath them, the boxes of screws have a pleasingly graphic quality. In Didi's workroom (right), a glass wall cabinet contains her collection of vintage Penguin paperbacks.

**Opposite:**
At one end of the workshop is an area that does double-duty as a potting shed. Still partly under construction, it has been constructed from found doors and old window frames. A view from the inside, showing one of the doors decorated by Patrick to amuse his four grandchildren.

**Above:**
A corner of the living room. Didi has
an art-school background, and both
she and Patrick have a good eye for
paintings and drawings. The portrait
of a girl was inherited from Didi's
father – a decorated commando
in the Second World War.

**Opposite:**
This sofa in the living room is one
that Patrick picked up on his travels.
Rather than reupholster it, the
couple have opted to throw a loose
plain cover over it, accessorized
with an ethnic-patterned cushion.

**Opposite:**

The barn, seen on a bleak winter's day. When the couple arrived in 1986, it was just four posts in the ground. Since then, it has been completely rebuilt in an 'L' shape, with a semi-enclosed courtyard and pond. The brick paving looks as if it has been there since the barn was first built, but is a new addition, laid by Patrick a few years ago.

**Above:**

These freestanding antique gates appear to have been arbitrarily added to the landscape – or left there. They function essentially as a folly, creating a focus while breaking up the view in a pleasing way.

# James Mitchell
## CLASSIC-CAR DEALER

Bicester Heritage in Oxfordshire is a former Second World War bomber station that is being sympathetically restored to house new businesses related to the classic-car industry. While walking around the site one day, I bumped into James, who was test-driving a Jaguar XK140. It was refreshing to see someone under 40 driving one of these beautiful cars.

We got to chatting, and he showed me round one of the buildings, the Blast House, where the Jaguar was usually stored and where he runs his business. Visiting it for the first time had been a case of love at first sight. Intrigued (or, as he says, 'blown away') by the name of the building, James knew as soon as he saw the glorious 1930s emerald engineering wall tiles that he had found the right place for his new business.

His love of old cars stemmed from his father, who had taught his son to drive in his 1930s MG PA. On leaving university – and unsure about what to do next – James began working for a classic-car dealer in one of the old mews in South Kensington. Once the hub of such dealerships in the 1950s, by the time he arrived the area had transformed into one of the wealthiest, most exclusive neighbourhoods in the world. A few of the old garages were still trading, however, and James began working for one of them – initially trusted only to wash and polish the old cars.

Such menial work might have put off some, but James says it was the best education he could have had. You only really get to know a car if you get up close, he says – and the best way to do that is to wash it.

**Above:**
The site of Bicester Heritage is
an old airfield, dotted about with
many hangars (left), measuring
around 11 m (36 ft)-high and 4,600
m² (50,000 sq ft). The Blast House
(right), with its huge, rolling steel
door, is unique as it is surrounded by
a second, half-height concrete wall,
built to deflect the blast of the most
powerful bombs.

**Opposite:**
One of the hangars on the site, originally built to house Bristol Blenheim bombers; today, there is only one of these light bomber aircraft left flying in the world. This hangar is currently sheltering a Tiger Moth from the 1930s.

**Above:**
Inside the Blast House, the walls are covered with distinctive emerald-green engineering tiles. Among the inhabitants are a white 1950s Jaguar XK140 (right), along with a red Aston Martin DB5, a blue Bristol 404 and an E-Type Jaguar (left).

# Hamish Black

## SCULPTOR

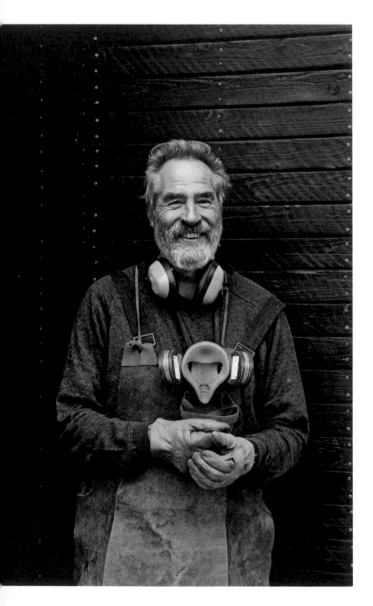

I passed this house many times, often on the way to the Jolly Sportsman pub, and have often wondered what the rusting hulks in the garden were. After a spot of local research, I found out that it was the home of Hamish Black, the sculptor. If you have not heard of him, you may have gazed through the hole in one of his creations on the Brighton seafront, a much-loved sculpture known as the 'doughnut' (its official title is *Afloat*) – an affectionate nickname bestowed by those who pass it every day is, after all, the greatest compliment that can be paid to a work of public art.

I met up with Hamish one winter's day. His wife had thoughtfully baked a banana cake, which, to my eyes, looked like a perfect sculpture, set in their Modernist house. The couple chanced upon their home 40 years ago, when a decaying 'For Sale' sign, half-concealed in the bushes, piqued their interest – a serendipitous find that sounds almost as if it had been scripted by the team behind a television property show.

The house was a wreck – just an industrial building and a barn – and in the intervening years the couple transformed the buildings, making full use of their architect son. Divided by sliding walls, the whole house can be opened up into a futuristic showcase for Hamish's work. Opposite the light, airy house, the industrial building has been converted into a studio, where he wields an oxyacetylene torch while working on his conceptual pieces. Some of these have found a home in the garden, giving it a surreal, unsettling air to passersby on the way to the pub.

**Above:**
The simplicity and hopeful optimism of a child's swing (left) contrasts with the imposing sculptures dotted around the garden (right). The work shown here is called *One World Series 2*, and is made out of steel that has been spot-welded together.

**Opposite:**
The house's modern silhouette contrasts wildly with the studio and the outside toilet, which appears to be in the process of being reclaimed by nature. In front of the house, two garden chairs have been pulled up to a table designed by Hamish.

**Overleaf**
In the main living room (p. 142), the floors are of polished concrete, with a Marcel Breuer-designed leather chair positioned in front of large picture windows that look out to the studio. The space is divided up by sliding partitions that control the size of the rooms and the play of light across Hamish's paintings. The clean, Modernist lines are broken up by carefully chosen pieces of furniture, including this antique dresser (p. 143), on top of which is a lovely birthday card from Hamish to his wife.

**Opposite:**
The kitchen is a good example of
how the couple make use of differing
styles that harmonize well together.
The units, made from a granite-
effect material, have an industrial
feel to them that contrasts with the
geometric artwork, the handthrown
plates on the wall and the antique
wooden chair.

**This page:**
Also in the kitchen, a rectangular
sliver of a window throws light onto
the work surface (left). Hamish's
studio (right), with a section of one
of his sculptures lying in front of a
wood-burning stove that the couple
use in the wintertime.

**Opposite:**
Because most of Hamish's sculptures are relatively large, he will start out by making a scale model. This particular model eventually became *Westminster Double*, a conceptual work that, when held at an acute angle and rotated, is revealed to be a map of Greater London.

**Above:**
Hamish at work in his studio (left). The amount of heavy lifting apparatus required to produce work that is often very subtle in meaning and texture is surprising (right).

# Tom Reeves
## PHOTOGRAPHER

My interest in the Reeves photography studio began when I first came to Lewes, in East Sussex. My visit coincided with a local exhibition, in which each shop in the high street displayed a black-and-white photo of the building as it was in the 1920s or '30s. All of the photographs had been shot on a pin-sharp plate camera, and together they formed a fantastic glimpse into everyday life in the town.

The photos had been taken by the Reeves studio, which itself is located on the high street. Edmund Reeves had set up his photography business in the town in 1858, and the shop and studio are still there today – now run by Edmund's great-grandson, Tom Reeves, and his wife Tania Osband. It is the oldest surviving photography studio in the world, with an archive of 150,000 glass plates and 100,000 negatives.

As fascinating as the archive is, I was also interested in the fabric of the building, a simple structure built in around 1870. Essentially a wooden lean-to, it has the most beautiful and flattering northerly light – which cannot be bettered, even in this age of digital cameras and technological gizmos. What is also unusual is that all of the ephemera related to running a photographic studio, from the negatives to the account books, some of it well over 150 years old, has been preserved.

The day I went to see Tom, he was about to photograph a four-month-old baby. The old maxim is, of course, 'never work with children or animals', but in Tom's case, it's just business as usual.

**Opposite:**
The lobby, where prospective subjects sit and wait to be called into the studio (for some, the feeling is akin to visiting the dentist). The photograph on the floor is a portrait of Tom with his studio lights. Above is a display of some of the 19th-century portrait photographs taken in the studio.

**Above:**
The door to the main studio (left). The whole room is panelled in wood, which gives it a wonderful hushed tone, and is perfect for relaxing prospective sitters. It still has many of its original fittings, including this light with a fluted glass shade (right).

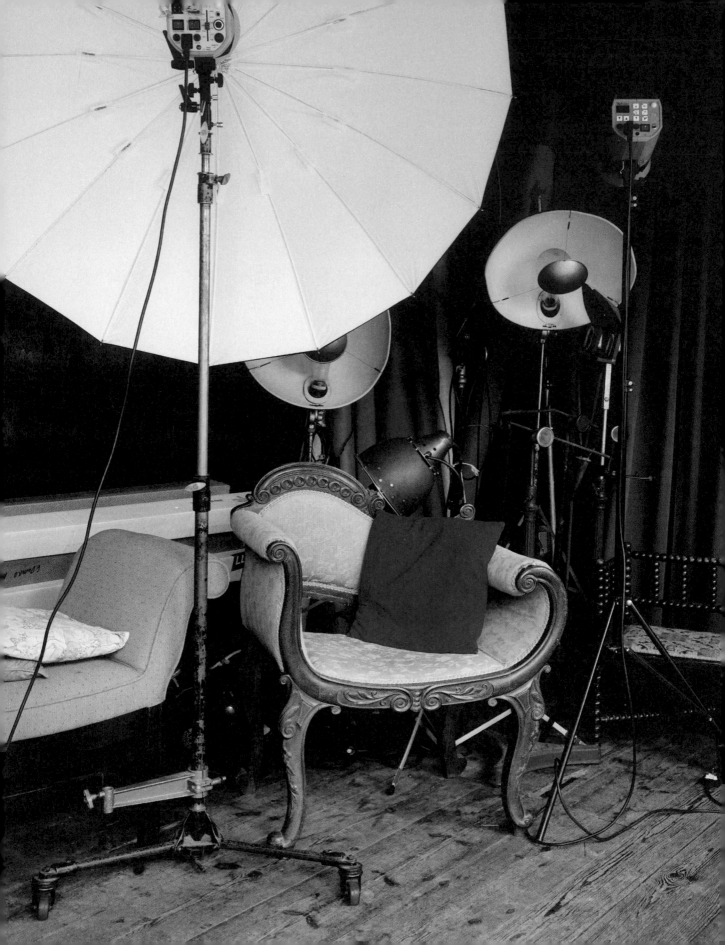

**Opposite:**
A corner of the studio, where a collection of lighting stands, metal dishes, reflectors and umbrellas are stored. The umbrellas are used to diffuse the light and make it more flattering. Also visible is a set of Colorama paper backdrops, which are used to tone with whatever each sitter is wearing.

**Above:**
Tom's collection of chairs dates back to the earliest days of studio, and many of them – along with much of the other furniture – have appeared as props across the generations of portraits taken at the studio. Cardboard boxes filled with rolls of Colorama backdrops are stacked against walls that still retain their original wood panelling.

# Hamish McKenzie

## ARTIST

Hamish McKenzie ('Mick') has lived on his houseboat (called *Dodge*, after the make of fire engine that forms part of the canopy) longer than almost anyone else on this stretch of river. It might look like a prop from a 1970s psychedelic fantasy film, but it is a real home that Mick built himself from an assortment of discarded odds and ends – including the fire engine.

Since arriving in Shoreham in 1986, he has spent most of his work time extending the lives of many of the historic vessels that he found here, including a significant collection of military craft from the Second World War. Sunken wrecks have become his speciality, and he derives great pleasure in refurbishing boats that are generally regarded as unsalvageable. Having just finished some major work on *Dodge*, Mick is now contemplating his next project: *Clive*, a Royal Canadian Navy motor torpedo boat that had lain on the bottom of the sea for 20 years.

I chanced on Mick's boat on an exceptionally hot July day. Although most of the houseboats along the towpath have a ramshackle charm, his stood out. I knocked gingerly on the door, and was met by a chap with a friendly face. Mick is generous with his time and is usually the first stop for people who need help with their boats. There seems to be no limit to his imagination and belief in what is possible in the world of boat-building, and the result is a curiosity that has been used for photoshoots by magazines such as Italian *Vogue* – although, Mick says, ruefully, he is still waiting for his copy.

**Opposite:**
This room is at the back of the boat, which is nearest the mooring (the front is made from a 1970s fire engine, while the middle section is an old motor coach). It has been modelled on the bow front of an old galleon, making it a perfect morning room, flooded with light.

**Above:**
Part of the main room formed by the old motor coach (left), where Hamish entertains guests and lodgers with his piano-playing. There is also a dartboard for those with less musical tastes. A passageway leads to the front of the boat (right), through a door filled with quirky Art Nouveau-inspired glass.

**Above:**
In terms of the decor, nothing is left
to chance, and there is a consistent
look that runs throughout Mick's
home – a good example of which
are the doors, with each having
its own character.

**Opposite:**
*Dodge* can be seen moored on the
River Adur in Shoreham at low tide.
Hamish has found many interesting
objects here over the last 30 years,
including a number of unexploded
bombs – now safely diffused and
stored at front of the boat.

# Steve Turner

## TIMBER-FRAMER

Steve Turner and his wife Jinks first stumbled upon their house nearly 30 years ago – 'house' being a loose description. In reality, it was a barn that had been completely flattened in the 1987 storm, so it was fortunate that Steve, a skilled timber-framer, had the skills to rebuild it – a task that would have been impossible had he stuck to his original plan of becoming an engineer specializing in plastics.

During the restoration, Steve found carpenters' marks that enabled him to date the building to 1600. Originally built to store grain for the large Elizabethan house next door, the barn has had various uses over the years, most recently to house cattle (with a separate 'bull pen', which Steve found still in evidence when he began the work). During the Second World War, the barn was commandeered for use as a laundry, as the main house was being used as a convalescent home for Canadian soldiers, and Steve found an old brick sink and a fire for the 'copper' used to wash the soldiers' sheets.

The carpentry techniques employed by timber-framers today are much the same now as they were in the Middle Ages, with each piece of wood cut and assembled in situ. Steve eschews modern aids and works only with hand tools, producing buildings untouched by digital design – a contemplative process that appeals to him. He picks up a scythe to illustrate his point. No one consciously 'designed' it, he says. In the hundreds of years since it was first used, its form has undergone only the subtlest of changes – a guiding principle for the way Steve runs his business.

**Above:**
A bunch of fading flowers still retain something of their beauty. These are in the main part of the barn, which is essentially one large room. Steve describes the restoration process as a work in progress – and that is after living there for almost 30 years.

**Opposite:**
A shelf in the study of Steve's wife, Jinks McGrath. A noted jewelry designer and maker, Jinks has written a number of books on jewelry design and also runs courses from a studio that Steve built for her.

**Opposite:**
As well as making furniture and restoring his home, Steve has put his tools to use by fashioning everyday objects. Everywhere you look, his work is in evidence; even something as simple and humble as a fruit bowl does not escape his attention.

**Above:**
The galley kitchen forms part of the main barn. Here, a collection of well-used pans, along with Jinks's collection of glassware, hangs above the Aga.

**Overleaf:**
Steve has cleverly divided up the mezzanine level of the barn into lots of different areas, each with its own character. One of these contains his study, complete with a writing slope and nicely patinated leather chair. Much of the main room has bookshelves, also built by Steve, which have the additional bonus of helping to insulate the space.

**Opposite:**
A traditional carpenter's workshop
is an intoxicating place, being
wonderfully atmospheric, with
its heady smell of wood glue and
sawdust. Housed in a separate
building, Steve's workshop contains
all of his hand tools and is big
enough to accommodate small jobs,
including this chair, which he is
in the process of restoring.

**Above:**
The workshop – not an electric drill
in sight. The chains are part of a
hoist, used to manoeuvre large beams
when Steve is working on them.

# Liam Watson
## MUSIC PRODUCER

I've always been intrigued by Toe Rag Studios in East London – just the name, for a start, grabbed my attention. It wasn't easy arranging to meet Liam Watson, the owner. He's not a man who bothers about emails, or even mobile phones, so it was great to meet up with him at last, one Friday morning in December.

The studio, famous for its analogue sound, is full of vintage musical equipment that Liam has collected over the past 20 years. In the early days of mobile phones and the Internet and just as music first went 'digital', he was tracking down microphones, tape decks and music consoles from old studios that were jettisoning them in favour of new technology. Liam was swimming against the tide and, as a result, his purpose-built studio attracts bands from all over the world in search of the old rock 'n' roll sound heard only on records from the 1960s and '70s (the White Stripes recorded their number-one selling album *Elephant* here).

When I arrived, Liam was busy splicing some tape together with a razor blade, wearing his customary attire of an old lab coat, which he likes to wear when working because it gives a clear visual distinction between the musicians and the producer. He rewound the tape and asked me what I thought of the band. Discussion quickly moved to the bass sound on Beatles records and whether the B-side of 'Anarchy in the UK' was better than the A-side. Although Liam's equipment is vintage, to say the least, his recording technique is essentially planted in the now – striving to give new, young bands that old, analogue sound.

**Above:**

Liam has a vast and enviable collection of vintage instruments, amplifiers and microphones – and these vintage drums made by Gretsch and Ludwig. Ludwig drums were made popular in the 1960s by Ringo Starr, while Charlie Watts of the Rolling Stones played a Gretsch drum kit. This one has a 'marine pearl' finish.

**Opposite:**

The equipment is stored in a room above the main recording studio, accessed by a very steep, narrow staircase. The floor is original 1950s lino; above it, the rack holds a Fender Tweed Deluxe amplifier, also from the 1950s. On the bottom shelf is a Vox Gyrotone rotating speaker; only two of these are known to exist in the world.

**Opposite:**

Liam is clear about his inspirations: the photo at the top is of Gerry and the Pacemakers; the one below shows Brian Poole and the Tremeloes. To the left is an advert for The Damned's first single, 'New Rose', a raw piece of noise that is very much in keeping with the studio's sound.

**Above:**

Just some of the equipment in the control room. Liam cites producers of the early 1960s as key influences, including Joe Meek, who set up his own studio above a shop in North London and recorded bands like The Tornados, whose instrumental 'Telstar' was – famously – Margaret Thatcher's favourite piece of music.

**Opposite:**
A Hammond organ in the band room, where musicians relax between takes. This type of organ produced the sound so famously used on Booker T. & the M. G.'s debut album *Green Onions*, released in 1962. Above it is a noticeboard hung with old badges, of the kind that used to be sewn onto haversacks, detailing the owners' travels.

**Above:**
The studio is found down a narrow alley in East London. The doorbell gives a flavour of what you will find when you enter: this DIY charm is in keeping with Liam's character. Visually, it is spare, but the focus is entirely on the music – part of the reason why musicians seek out Toe Rag's unique sound.

# Ian Hatton
## MOTORCYCLE DEALER

Ian Hatton first began working at Verralls, the oldest dealer in vintage and veteran motorcycles in the world, as a keen 19-year-old apprentice. Thirty years later, he is now the owner of this legendary company, having taken over in 2004 when the original owner, Brian Verrall, retired. (For those less versed in motorcycle terminology, 'vintage' refers to bikes built between 1915 and 1930, while 'veteran' motorcycles are those built even earlier.)

Previously located in Tooting in southwest London, the business has since relocated to a small village in West Sussex. Luckily, the new premises perfectly reflect the ethos of the firm. There is a harmony between the prewar motorcycles and the patina of the old buildings and workshops, and even the old petrol pump has always been there. Ian combines charm with a deep knowledge born of his long career in the business. When I met him, he was working on a Vincent motorcycle, still getting his hands dirty even though he is now the boss.

Our conversation turned to the thorny subject of restoration. The challenges of bringing a vintage motorcycle back to safe working condition are endless. How far do you go in removing decades of dirt before the patina of use is lost? Does introducing a new part to an old motorcycle affect the rest of it? Ian is firmly in the camp of preservation over restoration – or, to use his term, 'oily rag' – when a bike is not polished or 'bulled', but merely wiped with a rag to hold back the rust. A bike treated like this over many years gains a lustre that is impossible to replicate artificially.

**This page:**

The workshop and sales room. Verralls has a large double-fronted shop window on the road, but Ian chooses to display the bikes more discreetly round the back of the shop. Vintage and veteran motorcycles are an expensive business: Brian Verrall's collection was sold at Bonhams in 2008 for several hundreds of thousands of pounds.

**Opposite:**

To some, an engine – whether in a functioning motorcycle or just displayed on a shelf – is a thing of sculptural beauty. Ian shares the business with Gordon Button, who not only has an extensive knowledge of motorcycles, but is also an expert on Morgan three-wheelers – another speciality of the firm.

SUNBEAM MCC PIONEER RUN TO BRIGHTON 1975

SUNBEAM MCC PIONEER RUN TO BRIGHTON 1976

SUNBEAM MCC PIONEER RUN TO BRIGHTON 1977

SUNBEAM MCC PIONEER RUN TO BRIGHTON 1978

V.M.C.C. INTERNATIONAL WEST KENT 1986

V.M.C.C. INTERNATIONAL WEST 1987

1988

**Opposite:**
'Man cave' of dreams: the main
showroom. Over the years, Brian
Verrall amassed a huge collection of
motorcycle ephemera. On the walls
are old enamel advertising signs,
photographs of racers and a selection
of period motorcycle gear – just right
for accessorizing any new purchases.

**Above:**
A jumble of old exhaust pipes (left):
nothing here is thrown away. No
matter how damaged or beyond
repair it may at first appear, an
original part will always find a use –
even if it is just to provide a template
to make a new one. Many old tools
made the move with the business
from Tooting (right).

# Penny Rimbaud
# & Gee Vaucher
## MUSICIAN AND ARTIST

For those of a certain age, the term 'crass' may have a certain resonance – in a musical sense, that is. Formed in 1977, Crass the punk band cut a lonely path through the commercialism of the 1970s music industry, with its tribal sound and sophisticated graphics. The band's DIY approach extended to recording, packaging and selling its music through its own record label.

At the heart of all this activity was Dial House, a 16th-century farmhouse where the band lived between 1977 and 1984, and where Penny Rimbaud and Gee Vaucher still live today. While art students, they had roamed the countryside on Penny's motorbike, searching for a property, before spotting an advert in an estate agents' window in Ongar. From the start, they maintained an open-door policy – people just turned up and stayed. Fifty years later, this ethos is still intact.

The house is still a hub of artistic chaos, of whatever religious or political persuasion, but this nearly came to an end in the 1980s when a property developer decided to terminate the tenancy. A 12-year battle ended in the High Court, and the house was put up for auction. News spread and donations flooded in from around the world, enabling Penny and Gee to buy the house.

Today, Dial House is still a haven for artistic pursuits. Penny, with his scholarly air, could be mistaken for a retired don, rather than an ex-punk rocker, while Gee is the director of visual operations (she produced the defining look of the Crass records). She spends much of her time working in the garden, and seems proudest of the work they have created here.

**Previous pages:**
It is not easy to find the front door to Dial House. Access is around the back, through a wood-panelled anteroom with a curious mix of horse brasses, candles, corn dollies and ethnic lanterns (p. 186). In the kitchen, the dresser contains a selection of different teas and herbs (p. 187). Gee began producing her herbal remedies in the 1970s – an unusual activity at the time. Penny and Gee are strict vegetarians, and when I arrived Penny was stirring a large vegetable stew on the hob.

**Above:**
The wood panelling in the sitting room provides effective protection against draughts. It also harmonizes with the rest of the book-lined walls.

**Opposite:**
In the sitting room, the fireplace really is the hub of the house, with a kettle filled with water permanently warming on top of the freestanding wood-burning stove. In front of the fire is a small child's chair for sitting in while contemplating the flickering flames.

Penny Rimbaud & Gee Vaucher

**Opposite:**
On the landing, the bookshelf has
an unusual mix of sculpture and
typography balanced on top of it.
Collage and typography are Gee's
domain, with most of her artwork
containing one or both of these
elements. Her love of collage can be
seen to great effect on Crass's record
sleeves, and – for the more modern
age – in the band's brand identity.

**Above:**
Dial House has maintained an
open-door policy from the start,
with no locks on the doors and rooms
made available to guests – including
this one, with a Buddha-like figure
sitting in the fireplace. One visitor,
Steve Ignorant, arrived in 1977 and
stayed. Together, he and Penny
formed Crass (with Penny on drums)
to promote the ideals of Dial House.

**Opposite:**
When Penny moved here in 1967, the garden was a wilderness, with various outbuildings dotted about the place. With the arrival of Gee in 1968 and her expert skills, the garden was completely transformed. This wall is decorated with a collection of objects dug up or otherwise found in the grounds.

**Above:**
The garden is full of Native American Navajo references, including this totem pole-like structure (left). These continue inside the house: on the work surface in the kitchen is a Native American-influenced beaded coaster (right).

Penny Rimbaud & Gee Vaucher

**Below:**

Penny's study is an old clapboard
building in the middle of the garden.
At one end is a large window with a
desk in the corner; at the other is
a daybed. The study, with dictionary
and thesaurus prominently displayed,
could almost belong to an Oxbridge
don and reflects Penny's intellectual
approach to life.

**Opposite:**

The inhabitants of Dial House
have always practised a form of self-
sufficiency, with vegetable beds and
fruit trees dotted around the garden
(mainly through Gee's efforts). The
apples are destined to be pressed into
juice. The 1970s caravan is used as
accommodation when the house
and the other outbuildings are full.

**Below:**
Gee has carefully arranged seating around the garden, enabling it to be viewed and enjoyed from a number of different perspectives. Most of the structures in the garden were built by Penny, including this rotunda, complete with a Lloyd Loom chair inside.

**Opposite:**
The tree is one of the oldest in the garden, and was in a sorry state when the pair first moved here. Gee gradually nursed it back to health and shaped it, so that it now forms a natural canopy for the picnickers eating beneath its branches. The picnic table and benches were made by Gee out of railway sleepers.

# Alan Dodd

## ARTIST

The first time I saw Alan Dodd's house, standing at the end of an inauspicious lane in the Suffolk countryside, it took my breath away. I had first come across it on the blog The Bible of British Taste, written by Ruth Guilding. Built around 1640, the house (called 'Mustard Pot Hall' by the local children) is an exquisite jewel. It was conceived as a folly in the grounds of a manor house a mile away, but gradually became cut off from the main house and has stood alone ever since.

Hidden from the main road, it is not a building anyone would accidentally stumble upon. Alan was tipped off some 30 years ago by a friend he had met while studying at the Royal Academy in the 1960s. The purchase proved traumatic – a week before completion he received a phone call telling him that a local occult group had set fire to it. It was damaged but intact, so Alan negotiated a price reduction and moved in. The house has been an ongoing restoration, with Alan making subtle changes. The kitchen is a modern extension, but lattice windows from a nearby stable block were added to make it more in keeping with the main house.

Alan is a mine of information about the London art scene of the 1960s. He began his art education at Maidstone College of Art in 1958 at 15, and his first experience of life drawing involved sketching a youngish Quentin Crisp. He went on to study painting, and later specialized in murals. Some of his early commissions still exist – he laughs when he tells me that an Indian restaurant in Arundel still has a rococo ceiling that he painted in 1968.

**Opposite:**
Alan is a keen collector of china, and the dresser is full of his finds. Although the kitchen is housed in an extension added in the 1960s, by changing the windows and dressing the walls with taxidermy, Alan has created a room that blends in seamlessly with the rest of the house.

**Above:**
The house is not a hunting lodge, but there are hints that it might once have been and Alan's love of taxidermy is evident on several walls. The Chinese-style lattice windows were salvaged from a local stable block said to have been designed by James Wyatt, the architect of Fonthill Abbey.

**Overleaf:**
The main room in the house is actually the dining room. Above an antique sideboard hangs one of Alan's paintings, *Fonthill Abbey, after the Cattermole*, from 1974 (p. 202). It used to reside in his flat in London, but is now on permanent display here. The crystal chandelier hanging above an oval table does not look out of place in this humble folly (p. 203).

**Below:**

There is a delicate symmetry about Alan's house, even in the way he places his glassware. At New Year, he has friends to supper and the house is lit only by candles, adding to the pleasingly mysterious atmosphere.

**Opposite:**

Alan is tall and rangy, sporting a full beard, and is something of a 'natty' dresser – as evidenced by this pair of brogues, casually abandoned at the foot of a chair – preferring slightly worn tweed jackets and waistcoats, which give him a 'donnish' air.

**Opposite:**
In the exquisite guest bedroom on
the ground floor, towards the back
of the house, is a four-poster bed that
grazes the ceiling. Alan designed the
bed to incorporate a 17th-century
needlework panel, which now
serves as the headboard.

**Above:**
Even the bathroom cabinet is elegant
and reflects Alan's traditional style,
with old-fashioned shaving brushes
and a clothes brush on display, and
is accessorized with shells and an
urn containing dried flowers.

# Daniel

## ARTIST

I first photographed Daniel's treehouse five years ago. He gave me permission, but I never met him at the time. After a few phone calls, I found him still living here, half a decade later, in a field behind Plaw Hatch Farm, a 200-acre organic farm on the edge of the Ashdown Forest, in West Sussex. When he first arrived to work at the farm, Daniel didn't live on site. When he did start looking for somewhere to live, however, he found the original foundations of the treehouse – a few uprights set in concrete. These had been put in by the farm's cheese-maker, known simply as 'the Cheeseman', who had emigrated to Switzerland at short notice with a woman he had met on the farm.

The embryonic treehouse became Daniel's – with the Cheeseman's blessing. After reading a few books, Daniel cobbled together materials and built his new home for the grand total of £250. Its stability is down to the fact that it is actually supported by posts driven into the ground, rather than just being suspended in the branches. Since I last visited, Daniel has added a solar-powered battery and a gas cooker that costs him £30 a year to run. This is an exercise in cutting overheads to the bone: he pays his rent by working four days a month on the farm, spending the rest of the time running artistic workshops for children.

There is an irony that the charming simplicity of Daniel's lifestyle contrasts with the opulence of his closest neighbour – a vast manor house belonging to a vodka millionaire, who occupies it for a maximum of 10 weeks a year.

**Opposite:**
The treehouse has only one room, which is divided into different areas. This is effectively the 'living room', with an easy chair and books perched on rickety bookshelves. Daniel has a number of ukuleles that he plays when the evenings draw in. The walls are panelled in wood, with extra insulation added in some places.

**This page:**
Heat is provided by a wood-burning stove, which has recently been upgraded to meet health and safety standards. Next to the dartboard, Daniel has added stone-effect wallpaper to give the impression of a stone chimney.

**This page:**
A 1970s caravan in the 'garden', gradually being reclaimed by the undergrowth, provides additional storage. Daniel is self-taught, and learned how to build his home from a couple of books, using materials that were going spare on the farm.

**Opposite:**
To make the most of the limited space, Daniel has raised his bed off the ground. He now has electric light powered from a solar battery, rather than the more risky paraffin lamps he had been using before. The area underneath the bed doubles up as a place to dry laundry and additional storage for clothes.

# John & Diana Morley

## ARTISTS & NURSERY OWNERS

In 1972, John and Diana Morley were both struggling artists, just a few years out of art school. While at college, John had been lent a small cottage to paint in during the summer holidays in north Suffolk. The experience whet his appetite for the area, and that summer they began to look for a cottage of their own. Finding this house at the end of a long track, the couple began a long-term renovation which, in some respects, continues today.

After a successful period as a still-life painter, John's style fell out of fashion in the 1980s and he began hunting for a new way to make a living. Both he and Diana were keen gardeners, and their shared passion for snowdrops gradually evolved into a business. Thirty years later, theirs is the oldest nursery in the country selling snowdrops and is among the world's leaders in propagating and selling rare forms of this plant.

John and Diana started out with a few species supplied by the Rev. Richard Blakeway Phillips, a keen plantsman known to travel with his own trowel and poacher's pocket. Today, the garden has over 300 different varieties, which the couple sell via mail order. They began producing catalogues in 1984, now much prized and cherished by collectors, particularly the early editions, which are illustrated with John's drawings and paintings. Much of the profit from the business has been reinvested in the house – first they bought the cottage next door, and then built a Gothic-inspired room that, although completely different in style, harmonizes perfectly with the original buildings.

**Opposite:**
Gardening is in John's blood, as his grandfather was a gardener on a large estate and his parents had always gardened. The couple's own exquisite garden makes much use of sculptural box hedging to lend structure, along with antique garden furniture and statues.

**Above:**
John and Diana originally started out with one cottage, but managed to buy the one next door in the 1980s. They knocked through, and this is the end wall of the second cottage. A window and Juliet balcony have been added, giving the building a Tuscan feel that complements the restraint of the English garden.

**Overleaf:**
Diana is an artist in her own right, and this chair in her study (p. 220), covered with the stickers that used to be found on fruit in supermarkets, belonged to one of her artist friends. The stickers were randomly stuck onto the chair and then lacquered to preserve them. This is one of three chairs that the artist produced.

In the couple's small living room (p. 221), the fireplace, with granite surround, supports an artwork painted by another of their friends.

**These pages:**
Carefully chosen pieces of antique furniture have been mixed with the couple's own paintings and those of old art-school friends. John was bequeathed a large number of his own paintings many years ago by the original purchaser. The worn carpet on the stairs (opposite) is accessorized by piles of *World of Interiors* magazines.

**Overleaf:**
An unusual candelabra (p. 224) hangs above the staircase on the landing; a window in Diana's study (p. 225), which is at the front of the house. Diana, who paints under her maiden name of Howard, specializes in landscapes. She met John in 1969, while studying at the Royal Academy.

# Thomas & Angel Zatorski
## ARTISTS

I met Thomas Zatorski on a pontoon near Tower Bridge in London, a mooring that he built with the help of other vintage-boat owners. The project involved some battles with the local residents whose windows overlook it – and, indeed, the contrast could not be more apparent: a row of 1980s penthouse flats with balconies, synonymous with the yuppie excesses of the decade, when flats on the river were de rigueur, against Thomas's 122-year-old Dutch clipper, *De Walvisch*.

The boat is now a vessel for various artistic pursuits run under Thomas and his wife Angel's professional name, Zatorski + Zatorski. Thomas sees it as a living thing, and makes many analogies with the human body. He thinks conceptually, but there is no hint of pretension as he delivers his abstract ideas in a nonstop passionate rant. He wears an old bowler hat – perhaps a nod to the nearby City of London? – and a 1930s naval tunic, complete with braid.

Once on board, it becomes instantly clear that this boat is no grand folly. Everything has been designed and manufactured on site by Thomas. He befriended workers in boatyards in Holland and breakers who supplied him with original parts from submarines, and 'hoards' teak and English oak for future use. Although the couple and their three children live on board, they also use the boat as a hub for their 'happenings' – from a maritime opera that they conceived, designed and performed themselves, to artistic salons with guests gathered around the long table, a place for like-minded folk to meet and share food, drink and ideas.

**Opposite:**
Thomas bought the brass bulkhead light in the bathroom as a job lot; further examples can be found in other areas of the boat. The mirror, with its brass surround, may well be from a submarine. The walls have been painted in a shade of blue that Thomas chose particularly for its nautical feel.

**Above:**
Every detail has been carefully thought through, including the door to the bathroom, which is fitted with an old 'vacant–engaged' brass lock. Next to it is a series of antique brass light switches, which are in keeping with the rest of the fittings on board.

**Previous pages:**
Thomas and Angel's home contains a lot of taxidermy. But any feeling of morbidness at having stuffed animals about the place is lightened by the sense of theatricality found throughout the boat, as evidenced by the top hat and military jacket that Thomas is fond of wearing at the couple's artistic salons.

**Above:**

The theatricality of the couple's design sensibilities can be seen in this velvet Victorian chair, along with the low lighting and mahogany fittings. This anteroom is located at the front of the boat and leads into the master bedroom. Above the chair is an antique brass bulkhead light, which, like many of the fittings, came from another boat.

**Opposite:**

On board is a single, large room with a piano at one end, used at some of the couple's soirées (there is often a performance element to these evenings). On top of it is a stuffed reptile, and a stoat pelt is draped across the stool. This obsession with dead animals is echoed in Thomas's fascination with bones, which he calls 'nature's sculptures'.

**This page:**
The couple with their youngest son (right). The brass door hatch came from another boat, possibly a submarine (below left). The long table runs the length of the hold (below right).

**Opposite:**
Angel's collection of antique silver goblets and jugs is scattered across the boat. In the kitchen, the walls have been covered in blackboard paint. Whereas most kitchen noticeboards would have reminders like 'buy milk', this one records such important things to remember as '3 blasts – going to starboard' or '6 blasts – engine astern'.

# Steve Lowe

## ARTIST

Steve Lowe operates in a number of different guises. If he was in a band, he would probably be the drummer – shirking the limelight, but quietly busy keeping the beat. Although he is primarily a painter, Steve seems just as happy to promote other artists as he is pushing his own work. His career has evolved from running a small, independent book press to developing the press into a gallery, to being an agent representing artists that he likes. Money is not his main motivation – instead, he appears to be inspired by a streak of subversion that underlies most of his work. Being a provocateur, albeit a quiet one, is his raison d'être.

The building in which Steve lives and works has been owned by the same Italian family since the 1850s, and was once a workshop that made organs for funfairs. He has commandeered the whole of the basement as his amalgamated office, studio and living space, which he calls the 'L-13 Light Industrial Unit' – or, to give it its full name, 'L-13 Light Industrial Workshop and Private Ladies and Gentlemen's Club for Art Leisure and the Disruptive Betterment of Culture'. The 'L-13' part of the title came from a previous building he worked in, which was bombed by a Zeppelin L-13 in 1915.

Steve has a love–hate relationship with the art world, but is ultimately attracted to it for the potential to be subversive. He shies away from words like 'gallery' or 'agent', preferring to describe his role as to 'convert impractical artistic visions into reality, promote a playful polemic spirit, and irritate and offend delicate souls in the big bad world of culture and politics'.

31 ORGAN CHIAPPA LTD

CAS SECURITY

**These pages:**
The most important feature in Steve's 'kitchen' is the camping gas stove, which heats up the water for his coffee in the morning. This shares space with various paint-roller trays and a mirror that he uses to shave in. The kitchen bin appears to be hanging from the ceiling.

**Previous pages:**
'I chose oil paint because it smells, looks and feels organic and real, rather than plastic and fake,' Steve says. 'I also paint on humble dust sheets and hessian for the same reason.' He occasionally works with another painter under the name 'Harry Adams', chosen simply because it would always be first on the list of exhibitors.

**Opposite:**

Steve works at one end of the studio
with his assistant, Sophie, where
they coordinate the work of the
other artists they represent: Jimmy
Cauty (of The KLF), Billy Childish
(p. 10) and Jamie Reid, famous
for having designed all of the Sex
Pistols' record covers.

**Above:**

The painting studio. Steve studied
painting at art school, but drifted
into using sound, rather than
paint, to create what he calls 'noise
performances' (which, he says,
'everyone hated'). Moving into more
conventional bands for the next 15
years, he eventually tired of life as
a musician and returned to his first
love: painting and drawing.

# Corina Fletcher

## PAPER ENGINEER

Corina Fletcher and her husband Dominic live in a beautiful, traditional-style farmhouse, surrounded by gardens, an orchard and an assortment of barns and outbuildings. Visitors arriving for the first time immediately notice the grand scale of the windows and doors and period elegance of the façade. They appreciate the generous proportions that give the house its *Alice in Wonderland* air – and then they are told the story about how it came to be built there.

It started when the couple bought a lovely 16th-century farmhouse. Shortly after moving into their dream home, they went away for the weekend and returned to find it burned to the ground. Two years of legal wrangling and insurance claims later, they began again and the result is a farmhouse with a New England twist. Its size and elegant appearance make it appear as if it has always been there – or at least for a couple of centuries – while the sharp detail of outbuildings like the Tack Barn is a nod to contemporary design.

Corina, who trained as a graphic designer, is a successful paper engineer, designing books and gift products that pop up when you open them. She applies that same mix of artistic spirit and precision to the garden, which is largely her domain. While she works skilfully in three dimensions on her books, the fourth dimension – time – dominates the world of gardening. It is this seasonal effect that she finds so absorbing in her idyllic patch of England – the traumas of earlier events firmly in the past.

**Opposite:**
Fortunately, the fire did not destroy the infrastructure around the house, including the wonderful brick walls and barns that Corina retained to help shape the garden. There is also a pond large enough for a rowing boat; for a small fee, the couple's son will row you around it at one of the family's open-studio events in the summer.

**Above:**
The rear elevation of the Tack Barn (left), an old barn that has been refurbished and is now let to holiday-makers or to workers from the nearby Glyndebourne Festival. A rug dries on the line outside Corina's studio (right), which is located in another farm building, perched on top of stilts.

**Opposite:**
Although the front of the house is elegant and welcoming, with its central fig tree and balls of twisted willow made by craftsman and friend Dominic Parrette, curiously, everyone always uses the back door. The couple have also asked Dominic to make some willow screens and fences, which help to break up the garden into separate areas.

**Above:**
Leftover gourds from the garden (left). The lane leading up to the house is off a busy road and is shared with the local farmer (right). Once at the house, however, you are enveloped by the garden and it feels as if you are in the deepest countryside.

**This page:**
In the living room, the Victorian stuffed owl actually belongs to a friend, who is downsizing from a Scottish manse (above). The hallway leads to an open-plan dining room (right) – a quieter part of the house as most of the activity is centred around a huge table, originally from a monastery, in the kitchen. Found in an antiques shop, it has 12 drawers, each of which would have been allocated to a nun for storing her plate and cutlery.

**Opposite:**
In the bathroom, Corina's collection of coronation mugs are put to good use for storing makeup and toothbrushes. The mug on the right is a design by Eric Ravilious, and belonged to Dominic's grandmother.

**Opposite:**
Corina and some of the other parents taught themselves how to make the headdresses and props for their tiny local primary school's production of *The Lion King* from tissue paper and willow cane. After mastering the technique, they led workshops at the school so that the children could make some, too. These are some of the remaining lanterns.

**Above:**
Corina's studio is housed in what was originally the old granary, raised up on stilts, and located at the front of the house. The tools of a paper engineer's trade: a compass, paper folder and scalpel (left). To the right is an antique plan chest, in which she stores her work.

# Mark Wilson

## MUSICIAN

I was told about Mark Wilson by Gee Vaucher (p. 184). The pair have been friends since the late 1970s, when Mark's band The Mob supported Crass on a number of tours. In fact, it was the band's van that set Mark on the road he is on now. It was notorious for breaking down, and the repairs and maintenance work were left to him. As a result, he began collecting similar vans, so that he could rob them of parts and ensure that at least one working van was on the road at any given time.

In time the collection grew, the band folded and Mark – still in possession of the vans – decided to set up as a car breaker. He found an old quarry, and named the site Rockaway after 'Rockaway Beach', a song by his favourite band, The Ramones. Since then, Rockaway has become his home, and Mark has designed and built his own house here. The result is difficult to pin down in terms of architectural inspiration, since it has sprung fully formed from his fertile imagination.

The business feels like an extended family – when I arrived, there was a vat of lentil stew simmering on the hob and various friends and children buzzing around. It is also home to a number of businesses that work as a loose collective. Mark's daughter lives here, too, in an old traveller's wagon, and runs the revived music label All the Mad Men Records, which had originally issued Mark's LPs. The communal atmosphere is an important element of Rockaway, reminding Mark of all those squats in London he used to live in as a young musician, trying to make his way in the world.

Previous pages:
Mark's open-plan kitchen forms part of the main room of the house (p. 257). Food is often a communal affair, and a pot of vegan stew can usually be found bubbling away on the hob of the central island. In the rest of the room, old crates have been used as bookshelves; on the walls are promotional signs for a tattooist who works on site (p. 256).

**Above:**
A remnant from Mark's old 1960s Bedford CA delivery van, now ceremoniously attached to the wall, above a set of mirrors. Below is an L-shaped sofa, scattered with cushions from Mexico.

**Opposite:**
The back door to Mark's chalet-style house, which is built at the very edge of a quarry. He describes living at Rockaway as a 'junkyard in a forest', which is, in some ways, a fairly accurate description.

**Opposite:**
Mark's daughter also lives on site in this traveller's caravan, with an alloy exterior, not dissimilar to an American Airstream. The kitchen has its original 1950s cooker, as well as grained Formica cabinets and walls to match.

**Below:**
The rest of the caravan is panelled in wood, with built-in cupboards. The original fireplace, with mantelpiece matched to the walls, has alloy panels that reflect the heat back into the room. To the left is a 1930s upholstered club chair, with a Native American-style blanket thrown over it.

**Previous pages:**
At first, Rockaway does resemble a junkyard, but on closer inspection, it is revealed to be a hive of industry with many companies working from business units that Mark built and then let. He uses the huge barn as a breakers' yard, the core business at Rockaway. On the day I arrived, there were around 10 Tesco delivery vans, all waiting to be dismantled. 'The yard is my canvas,' Mark says, 'and the forklift my paintbrush.'

# Robert Hayward

## ANTIQUES DEALER

Robert Hayward's interest in and knowledge of materials and how they are affected by place or situation has been honed over the last three decades as an antiques dealer and informs his business today. Soon after completing a degree in sculpture, he helped some friends with a few house clearances and was shocked at the number of objects he saw being discarded. He decided to rescue some of them to restore and sell on himself – a practise he calls 'skip-diving'.

Successful skip-diving led to renting a stand at Ardingly Antiques Fair (near Haywards Heath, in West Sussex) and eventually to this shop in Lewes, which he bought with his wife Dee. Gradually, Rob began to specialize in antique mirrors, and his artistic training has come in useful as the shop doubles as a workshop, where he carries out repairs. Rob explains that many people avoid this market, believing that mirrors are fragile, but he says that in 35 years he hasn't broken one yet. After saying this, he pauses and adds wryly that he hopes he hasn't jinxed things.

Today, Rob only buys things that he likes, rather than seeking out items he thinks will sell easily – and notes, chuckling, that even after many years in the trade, this probably isn't the soundest basis for a business. Cliffe Gallery Antiques can be found at the end of Cliffe High Street in Lewes in East Sussex. If you visit on a Saturday, you will be sure to meet many of the town's cast of characters, as Rob knows them all.

**Opposite:**
Rob and Dee effectively live above
the shop, which they bought in
2000, just before the town suffered
severe flooding. With the help of
timber-framing expert Steve Turner
(p. 160), Rob transformed the retail
space, which doubles as a makeshift
workshop, where he repairs mirrors
while customers browse.

**Above:**
Although Rob specializes in mirrors,
he also deals in anything that he
particularly likes, including this
antique porcelain urn, seen next to
a bunch of ceramic flowers (left). In
the living room, the walls have been
painted a powdery yellow. One of
Rob's mirrors perches on top of the
mantelpiece, along with a bunch
of dried flowers (right).

**This page:**
Rob can turn his hand to most repairs. Using the shop as a workshop gives the business an authenticity that other galleries, where the antiques are polished and presented as the finished product, can't match. The smell of wood glue and sawdust also adds to the ambience.

**Opposite:**
Some of the plastered walls have been left unpainted, with oak panels attached that echo the beams in the ceiling. Here, a couple of mirrors await collection at the back of the shop, together with an antique rocking horse that will soon be needing Rob's attention.

**Opposite:**

The first floor of the house is divided into three rooms: a kitchen at the back and living room at the front, with the dining room – a relatively low, long room – in between. In this room, a Welsh dresser houses Dee's collection of antique china and some of the scarves that are always wound around Rob's neck.

**Above:**

The entrance to the house (see p. 264) is at the back. Leading up to the first floor is a very old staircase, lined with a collection of mirrors and paintings, which was rescued by Rob many years ago from a skip. At the top is a light well, which floods the area below with natural light.

**Above:**
On the second floor are the house's
three bedrooms. In the master
bedroom is a bedside table in the
shape of a classical Doric column;
above it are photographs of two of
the couple's children when they
were young.

**Opposite:**
A classical bust adorns the landing
on the way up to the second floor. All
of the walls have been painted white,
with the roof beams given the same
treatment. Because the sweep of the
staircase is so tight, Rob has cleverly
used some nautical rope and brass
rings, rather than having to fashion
a wooden banister rail.

**Opposite:**

The glazed rear wall of the house allows in plenty of light, effectively turning the kitchen into a morning room. The sink has the appearance of a work in progress, with various tiles awaiting their turn to be fixed to the wall. Rob whitewashed the beams and wooden beading that holds the window panes in place.

**Above:**

In the bathroom, the beams and walls have also been whitewashed. The bath is an antique with its original fittings, and is accessorized with houseplants, candles and a jar full of seashells.

# Alison Morris
## JOURNALIST AND ARTIST

Endlings is an eclectic shop selling 'paintings, prints, books and things', located in the Old Town section of Hastings, on the south coast. It is run by Alison Morris, an artist, printmaker and journalist, and her partner Paul, both of whom are also avid collectors – so avid, in fact, that the shop's stock is mostly drawn from the couple's personal possessions.

When they started to run out of space at home, Alison and Paul didn't make the usual phone call to a storage company, but instead found an empty retail space and decided to use it for selling and storing their work and collections. It also functions as Alison's workshop and writing studio. 'I guess the whole point is the reality of how we live,' she admits. 'A good proportion of all this frenzied collecting has been funded by a career writing about architectural minimalism – an irony that is not lost on me.'

I first stumbled across Endlings after being forwarded one of their Instagram posts. On my first visit, I left with a stunning Austrian botanical print of a dandelion. On my next, I visited the couple's charming Victorian house nearby. Alison's point about the irony of a lifetime of collecting paid for by a career writing about minimalism is apt: the house is a minimalist's nightmare. The couple trawl auctions and focus on forgotten genres (such as overlooked female British artists from the 1920s). Every inch of space, including the walls, has been crammed full of pictures, antiques, books, blankets and furniture, all of which reflect Alison and Paul's personalities and interests.

**Opposite:**

This 1930s store cupboard housing antique crockery is painted in a wonderful shade of eau de nil, a fashionable colour of the decade. It was a present from Paul to Alison – a hugely romantic gift that is also a fantastic example of how something as mundane as a cupboard can be both practical and beautiful.

**Above:**

In the kitchen, stacks of old books are piled up on the table and original works by lost or forgotten artists line the walls. A pew has been pushed up against one wall, and a shelf above the picture rail runs all the way round the room – ideal for propping up more paperbacks and cookbooks.

**Overleaf:**

Alison was originally keener to live in an area a few miles from Hastings, and it was Paul who insisted that they view this house in the Old Town – a delightful Victorian building with generous bay windows and plenty of original features. It was love at first sight, and they bought the house that same day. In the living room (p. 280), the original carved mantelpiece is loaded up with yet more books. Another room in the house (p. 281) contains Ercol furniture from the 1950s: one chair has been 'reupholstered' with old blankets; another has a stack of Welsh blankets piled on top of it.

**This page:**
In the living room are some of
Alison's favourite things, including
plenty of books, an ebony pineapple,
two African-inspired ceramic vases
and portraits and paintings that may
well find themselves on the shelves
of the shop in the future.

**Above:**
The entrance to Endlings, the couple's shop/office/studio in Courthouse Street. It's not only paintings or drawings that you'll find in there, as you are just as likely to come across a rug or a lamp – as long as it is in keeping with Alison and Paul's particularly British postwar aesthetic.

**Overleaf:**
In the bedroom, Paul's Victorian chest of drawers groans beneath the weight of a pile of books (p. 284). Perched on top are a relief map of Iceland and a Meccano advertising sign from the 1950s. In the shop (p. 285), the two exquisitely printed German wall hangings would have been used in a school in the 1950s.

**These pages:**

More 'finds' cover the couple's bedroom walls. The couple used to trawl auction houses for their treasures, but since having the shop, they have found that people come to them. Nothing is sacred: their house acts as a holding bay for things that may, eventually, move into the shop once space becomes available. When I visited Endlings, someone came in with several dusty portfolios, explaining that they were clearing out their father's house and had found some of his drawings and paintings from his time at St Martins School of Art in the 1950s. In this respect, Alison and Paul are helping to preserve works of art that would otherwise have been lost forever.

**HAMISH BLACK** — 138
hamishblack.com

**BILLY CHILDISH** — 10
williamhamper.com
twitter.com/childishinfo

**DANIEL** — 210
Plaw Hatch Farm,
East Grinstead, West Sussex
plawhatchfarm.co.uk
instagram.com/plawhatchfarm

**ALAN DODD** — 198
alandodd.co.uk

**VIV & BEN ENGLISH** — 76
English's Electric Tattoo,
18a Malling Street, Lewes,
East Sussex BN7 2RD
facebook.com/englishselectrictattoo
instagram.com/englishelectrictattoo

**CORINA FLETCHER** — 244
Upper Lodge, The Broyle, Ringmer,
East Sussex BN8 5AP
upperlodgesussex.com
instagram.com/upperlodgesussex

**PATRICK HALL** — 122
instagram.com/inglishallantiques

**PETER HALL** — 34
Breaky Bottom Vineyard,
Whiteway Lane, Lewes,
East Sussex BN7 3EX
breakybottom.co.uk

**ANTHONY & LORI
INGLIS HALL** — 88
instagram.com/inglishallantiques
loriandthecaravan.co.uk

**JONNY HANNAH** — 24
instagram.com/darktownresident

**IAN HATTON** — 178
Verralls, The Old Forge, Quicks Yard,
Handcross, West Sussex RH17 6BJ
verralls.com

**ROBERT HAYWARD** — 264
Cliffe Gallery Antiques,
39 Cliffe High Street, Lewes,
East Sussex BN7 2AN

**CHRIS LEWIS** — 110
South Heighton Pottery,
South Heighton, Newhaven,
East Sussex BN9 0HL
chrislewisceramics.com

**STEVE LOWE** — 236
L-13 Light Industrial Workshop,
31 Eyre Street Hill, Clerkenwell,
London EC1R 5EW
l-13.org
instagram.com/
l13lightindustrialworkshop

**HAMISH McKENZIE** — 154
'Houseboat Dodge',
River Adur, Shoreham-by-Sea,
West Sussex
bloominadur.co.uk/boats

**JAMES MITCHELL** — 132
Pendine Classic Cars,
The Blast House, Bicester Heritage,
Buckingham Road, Bicester,
Oxfordshire OX27 8AL
pendine.co
instagram.com/pendinehistorics

**JOHN & DIANA MORLEY** — 216
North Green Snowdrops,
North Green Only, Stoven, Beccles,
Suffolk NR34 8DG
northgreensnowdrops.co.uk

**ALISON MORRIS** — 276
Endlings, 3BS, 12 Courthouse Street,
Hastings, East Sussex TN34 3BA
instagram.com/endlings.hastings

**TOM REEVES** — 148
Edward Reeves Photography,
159 High Street, Lewes,
East Sussex BN7 1XU
edwardreeves.com
reevesarchive.co.uk

**PENNY RIMBAUD
& GEE VAUCHER** — 184
Dial House, Epping, Essex
onoffyesno.com

**LISA SMALLPEICE** — 46
Hawthbush Farm, Gun Hill,
Heathfield, East Sussex TN21 0JY
hawthbushfarm.co.uk
gunbrewery.co.uk
amlybotanicals.com
instagram.com/amlybotanicals

**CAROLYN TRANT** — 100
carolyntrantparvenu.blogspot.co.uk
thepf.co.uk

**STEVE TURNER** — 160
Streat Place Barn, Streat, Ditchling,
East Sussex BN6 8RU
thedairyatstreatplacebarn.co.uk

**SARAH WALTON** — 62
Keepers, Bo Peep Lane, Alciston,
Polegate, East Sussex BN26 6UH
sarahwalton.co.uk
instagram.com/sarahwceramics

**LIAM WATSON** — 170
Toe Rag Studios, 166a Glynn Road,
Clapton, London E5 0JE
toeragstudios.com

**MARK WILSON** — 254
Rockaway Park,
Temple Cloud, Somerset
rockawaypark.co.uk
instagram.com/rockawaypark.co.uk

**THOMAS & ANGEL ZATORSKI** — 226
The Cultureship,
CC2, Trinity Buoy Wharf,
Orchard Place, London E14 0JY
thecultureship.org
zatorskiandzatorski.com